Hermit C

Story by Beverley Randell
Illustrated by Julian Bruere

Hermit Crab is at home.
She is inside a shell.
She is too big
for this little shell.

3

Hermit Crab
is looking for a **big** shell.

This shell is big.
Hermit Crab will look inside.

Oh, no!

A big Hermit Crab is inside.

Here comes a fish,
a big hungry fish.
He likes to **eat** Hermit Crabs!

9

Help! Help! Help! Help!
Where is a home
for Hermit Crab?

This is a big shell.
This is a good home
for Hermit Crab.
She is going inside.

Go away, big hungry fish.
Go away, oh go away!
Hermit Crab is not for you.
She is not for you today.

Hermit Crab is **safe**.